100

QUOTES
THAT WILL
CHANGE YOUR
LIFE

D1527863

LIBRARY MINDSET

"Some people die at 25 and aren't buried until 75."

-Benjamin Franklin

#1

"If your only goal is to become rich, you will never achieve it."

-John D. Rockfeller Sr.

#2

"When people talk, listen completely. Most people never listen."

-Ernest Hemingway

#3

"Better to jump and make a mistake than sit there too frightened to make a move."

-Richard Templar

#4

"If you are comfortable dancing in public without alcohol or drugs, you are at peace with who you are."

-Ankur Warikoo

#5

"People do not decide their futures, they decide their habits and their habits decide their futures."

-F.M. Alexander

#6

"Never put too much trust in friends, learn how to use enemies."

-Robert Greene

#7

"Only staying active will make you want to live a hundred years."

-Japanese Proverb

#8

"You are what you eat and read."

-Maya Corrigan

#9

"**Fall in love with taking care of yourself. Fall in love with becoming the best version of yourself but with patience, with compassion and respect to your own journey.**"

-S. Mcnutt

#10

"The first step toward getting somewhere is to decide that you are not going to stay where you are."

-J.P. Morgan

#11

"The single most powerful asset we all have is our mind. If it is trained well, it can create enormous wealth."

-Robert T. Kiyosaki

#12

"Learn to choose your mental health over old attachments."

-Hana Shebar

#13

"If it isn't a clear yes, then it's a clear no."

-Greg McKeown

#14

"Procrastination will delay your dreams."

-Vex King

#15

"**Reading an hour a day is only 4% of your day. But that 4% will put you at the top of your field within 10 years. Find the time.**"

-Patrick Bet-David

#16

"May God have mercy upon my enemies, because I won't."

-George S. Patton

#17

"Surround yourself only with people who are going to lift you higher."

-Oprah Winfrey

#18

"If you cannot decide, the answer is no."

-Naval Ravikant

#19

"You'll never find a rainbow if you're looking down."

-Charlie Chaplin

#20

"Always say less than neccessary."

-Robert Greene

#21

"It always seems impossible, until it is done."

-Nelson Mandela

#22

"Remember, some of the best times of your life haven't even happened yet."

-Doug Carwright

#23

"A ship is safe in harbor, but that's not what ships are built for."

-John A. Shedd

#24

"**When a person can't find a deep sense of meaning, they distract themselves with pleasure.**"

-Victor Frankl

#25

"A man who fears suffering is already suffering from what he fears."

-Montaigne

#26

"We work jobs we hate, to buy things we don't need, to impress people we don't like."

-Tyler Durden

#27

"Your time is limited so don't waste it living someone else's life."

-Steve Jobs

#28

"A friend to all is a friend to none."

-Aristotle

#29

"By changing nothing, nothing changes."

-Tony Robbins

#30

"If you're serious about changing your life, you'll find a way. If not you'll find an excuse."

-Jen Sincero

#31

"Your life does not get better by chance, it gets better by change."

-Jim Rohn

#32

"Change is hard at first, messy in the middle and gorgeous at the end."

-Robin Sharma

#33

"You will face many defeats in life but never let yourself be defeated."

-Maya Angelou

#34

"If you want a new idea, read an old book."

-Ivan Pavlov

"If you can change your mind, you can change your life."

-William James

#36

"If people are not laughing at your goals, your goals are too small."

-Azim Premji

#37

"If you are lonely when you're alone you are in a bad company."

-Jean Paul Sartre

#38

"We suffer more in imagination than in reality."

-Seneca

#39

"When you have something to say, silence is a lie."

-Jordan B. Peterson

#40

"The oldest, shortest words - 'yes' and 'no' - are those which requires the most thought."

-Pythagoras

#41

"In life, the only two things you can control are your effort and your attitude. Everything else is not up to you."

-S. Mcnutt

#42

"Do what you can, with what you have, where you are."

-Theodore Roosevelt

#43

"The way to get started is to quit talking and begin doing."

-Walt Disney

#44

"If you live each day as if it were your last, someday you'll be right."

-Steve Jobs

#45

"Don't judge each day by the harvest you reap but by the seeds that you plant."

-Robert Louis Stevenson

#46

"The only impossible journey is the one you never begin."

-Tony Robbins

#47

"The best revenge is not to be like your enemy."

-Marcus Aurelius

#48

"Everyone must choose one of two pains: The pain of discipline or the pain of regret."

-Jim Rohn

#49

"Never spend money before you have it."

-Thomas Jefferson

#50

"The poor and the middle class work for money. The rich have money work for them."

-Robert T. Kiyosaki

#51

"He who has a why to live for can bear with almost any how."

-Friedrich Nietzsche

#52

"I'd rather be optimistic and wrong than pessimistic and right."

-Elon Musk

#53

"Everyone thinks of changing the world but no one thinks of changing himself."

-Leo Tolstoy

#54

"One day you will wake up and there won't be any more time to do things you've always wanted. Do it now."

-Paulo Coelho

#55

"You should examine yourself daily. If you find faults, you should correct them. When you find none, you should try even harder."

-Israel Zangwill

#56

"If you set your goals ridiculously high and it's a failure, you will fail above everyone else's success."

-James Cameron

#57

"Travel and tell no one, live a true love story and tell no one, live happily and tell no one, people ruin beautiful things."

-Kahlil Gibran

#58

"The nearer a man comes to a calm mind, the closer he is to strength."

-Marcus Aurelius

#59

"The first principle is that you must not fool yourself and you are the easiest person to fool."

-Richard Feynman

#60

"Discipline is choosing between what you want now and what you want most."

-Abraham Lincoln

#61

"Step out of your comfort zone and face your fears. Growth takes place when you are challenged, not when you are comfortable."

-Vex King

#62

"Be so good that they can't ignore you."

-Steve Martin

#63

"Who chases two rabbits catches neither."

-Japanese Proverb

#64

"When you focus on you, you grow. When you focus on shit, shit grows."

-Unknown

#65

"The journey of a thousand miles begins with a single step."

-Lao Tzu

#66

"A little impatience will spoil great plans."

-Chinese Proverb

#67

"You've made mistakes in the past, you will probably make more in future. And that's ok."

-Hanna Shebar

#68

"When something is important enough, you do it even if the odds are not in your favor."

-Elon Musk

#69

"A good plan, violently executed now, is better than a perfect plan next week."

-George S. Patton

#70

"Good habits formed at youth make all the difference."

-Aristotle

#71

"If you want to conquer fear, don't sit home and think about it. Go out and get busy."

-Dale Carnegie

#72

"A problem is a chance for you to do your best."

-Duke Ellington

#73

"A fit body, a calm mind, a house full of love. These things cannot be bought - they must be earned."

-Naval Ravikant

#74

"No mortal man, is wise at all moments."

-Pliny The Elder

#75

"If a man knows not to which port he sails, no wind is favorable."

-Seneca

#76

"Life will not postpone our death. So, let us not postpone our life"

-Unknown

#77

"Win through your actions, never through argument."

-Robert Greene

#78

"Motivation is what gets you started. Habit is what keeps you going."

-Jim Rohn

#79

"Learn from the mistakes of others... you can't live long enough to make them all yourselves."

-Chanakya

#80

"The greatest glory in living lies not in never falling, but in rising every time we fall."

-Nelson Mandela

#81

"The only way to do great work is to love what you do."

-Steve Jobs

#82

"He will never have true friends who is afraid of making enemies."

-William Hazlitt

#83

"A man who is a master of patience is master of everything else."

-George Savile

#84

"Inaction breeds doubt and fear. Action breeds confidence and courage."

-Dale Carnegie

#85

"No man ever steps in the same river twice, for it's not the same river and he's not the same man."

-Heraclitus

#86

"Don't let yourself be controlled by three things: people, money, or past experience."

-Unknown

"Do what is right, not what is easy nor what is popular."

-Roy T. Bennett

#88

"The goal is not to be better than the other man, but your previous self."

-Dalai Lama

"The future depends on what you do."

-Mahatma Gandhi

#90

"We have two ears and one mouth, so we should listen more than we say."

-Zeno

#91

"The bigger the 'why' the easier the 'how'."

-Jim Rohn

#92

"The only man who never makes mistakes is the man who never does anything."

-Theodre Roosevelt

#93

"We're what we repeatedly do. Excellence, therefore, is not an act, but a habit."

-Aristotle

#94

"If you quit once it becomes a habit. Never quit!"

-Michael Jordan

#95

"**When a person dies, he leaves his belongings at home, his family at the graveside and the only thing that accompanies him are his deeds.**"

-Unknown

#96

"Waste no more time arguing about what a good man should be. Be one."

-Marcus Aureilius

#97

"Live as if you were to die tommorrow. Learn as if you were to live forever."

-Mahatma Gandhi

#98

"Twenty years from now you will be more disappointed by the things that you didn't do than by the ones you did do."

-H. Jackson Brown Jr.

#99

"One moment can change a day, one day can change a life and one life can change the world."

-Buddha

#100

Made in United States
North Haven, CT
28 August 2023

40828568R00064